Practical Benchmarking for Mutual Improvement

The Management Master Series

William F. Christopher
Editor-in-Chief

10

Practical Benchmarking for Mutual Improvement

Carl G. Thor

PRODUCTIVITY PRESS

Portland, Oregon

Volume 10 of the *Management Master Series*
William F. Christopher, Editor-in-Chief
Copyright © 1995 by Productivity Press, Inc.

Productivity Press
P.O. Box 13390
Portland, OR 97213-0390
United States of America
Telephone: 503-235-0600
Telefax: 503-235-0909

ISBN: 1-56327-075-7

Book and cover design by William Stanton
Cover illustration by Paul Zwolak
Typeset by Laser Words, Madras, India
Printed and bound by BookCrafters in the United States of America

Library of Congress Cataloging-in-Publication Data

Thor, Carl G.
    Practical benchmarking for mutual improvement / Carl G. Thor.
      p.   cm. – (Management master series; v. 10)
    Includes bibliographical references.
    1. Benchmarking (Management) I. Title. II. Series.
    HD62.15.T53   1995   94-24001
    658.5'62–dc20   CIP

00 99 98 97 96 95   10 9 8 7 6 5 4 3 2 1

—CONTENTS—

Publisher's Message   vii

1. **Introduction to Benchmarking   1**
   What Is Benchmarking?   1
   Misconceptions about Benchmarking   2
   Benchmarking and Measurement   4

2. **Types of Benchmarking   5**
   Internal Benchmarking   5
   Industry Study   6
   Business Process: Exchange Model   7
   Business Process: Group Model   8

3. **Subjects of Benchmarking   10**
   Financial Data   10
   Nature of Product/Service   11
   Operational Practices/Equipment   11
   Process/Department Descriptions   12
   Operational Metrics   13

4. **Benchmarking Example: Industry Study   16**
   Finding Participants   17
   Planning the Study   17
   Survey Development   18
   Processing and Interpretation   22
   Response to Survey Findings   24

5. **Benchmarking Example:**
   Process (Exchange Model) **26**
   Getting Started   26
   Information Base   29
   Process Template   31
   Outside Comparisons   34
   Implementing Change   37

6. **Summary and Conclusion** **39**

Notes   41
Further Reading   42
About the Author   43

PUBLISHER'S MESSAGE

The *Management Master Series* was designed to discover and disseminate to you the world's best concepts, principles, and current practices in excellent management. We present this information in a concise and easy-to-use format to provide you with the tools and techniques you need to stay abreast of this rapidly accelerating world of ideas.

World-class competitiveness requires managers today to be thoroughly informed about how and what other internationally successful managers are doing. What works? What doesn't? and Why?

Management is often considered a "neglected art." It is not possible to know how to manage before you are made a manager. But once you become a manager you are expected to know how to manage and to do it well, right from the start.

One result of this neglect in management training has been managers who rely on control rather than creativity. Certainly, managers in this century have shown a distinct neglect of workers as creative human beings. The idea that employees are an organization's most valuable asset is still very new. How managers can inspire and direct the creativity and intelligence of everyone involved in the work of an organization has only begun to emerge.

Perhaps if we consider management as a "science" the task of learning how to manage well will be easier. A scientist begins with an hypothesis and then runs experiments to observe whether the hypothesis is correct. Scientists depend on detailed notes about the experiment — the timing, the ingredients, the amounts — and carefully record all results as they test new hypotheses. Certain things come to be known by this method; for instance, that water always consists of one part oxygen and two parts hydrogen.

We as managers must learn from our experience and from the experience of others. The scientific approach provides a model for learning. Science begins with vision and desired outcomes, and achieves its purpose through observation, experiment, and analysis of precisely recorded results. And then what is newly discovered is shared so that each person's research will build on the work of others.

Our organizations, however, rarely provide the time for learning or experimentation. As a manager, you need information from those who have already experimented and learned and recorded their results. You need it in brief, clear, and detailed form so that you can apply it immediately.

It is our purpose to help you confront the difficult task of managing in these turbulent times. As the shape of leadership changes, The *Management Master Series* will continue to bring you the best learning available to support your own increasing artistry in the evolving science of management.

We at Productivity Press are grateful to William F. Christopher and our staff of editors who have searched out those masters with the knowledge, experience, and ability to write concisely and completely on excellence in management practice. We wish also to thank the individual volume authors; Diane Asay, project manager; Julie Zinkus, manuscript editor; Karen Jones, managing editor; Bill Stanton, design and production management; Susan Swanson, production coordination; Laser Words, text and graphics composition.

Norman Bodek
Publisher

1

INTRODUCTION TO BENCHMARKING

People have been making comparisons since before recorded time. Tribal executives, having noted that cooked meat tastes better than raw meat, sent out an early benchmarking team to improve their "meat processing techniques." The team came back with fire! A great deal of benchmarking on price takes place in exotic bazaars and in shopping centers alike. Tools that individuals use comfortably in their homes often are brought to work. So finally organizations are interested in improving their abilities to compare products and processes. This book brings systematic thinking about comparison to an area where previously the superior judgment of a single expert was the driver.

WHAT IS BENCHMARKING?

Benchmarking in organizations is *the systematic comparison of elements of performance in an organization against those of other organizations, usually with the aim of mutual improvement.*

Systematic comparison is not mainly accidental or serendipitous. Those involved express their intention first, then gather data and interpret it with care. A consequent improvement flows from the exercise.

The elements of performance to compare can be quite different from organization to organization. Some organizations look for a more durable product, others want faster processing and/or fewer errors, others emphasize cost. The organization in question can be any size or type. It can be a whole company or a government agency, a division or branch, a cross-cutting business process, or a small work group. Finally, the way an organization gets help from another organization is usually to offer mutual help to them in the same or another field.

Other narrower approaches to benchmarking, though perfectly legitimate and useful, keep an organization from getting maximum potential value out of their comparison exercises. For example, some benchmarkers think that if you don't compare yourself to a world-class organization, you run the risk of setting far too easy a goal. They think that benchmarking is the way to get ten times the improvements; that a mere doubling of performance is not worthy.

There are only two problems with this thinking. First, no organization is world-class. Only business practices, processes, and approaches are world-class. No single organization is best at everything, or even pretty good at everything. Any organization can have weaknesses, perhaps lulled by intimations of immortality lent by quality awards and the like. If a true, best practitioner can be located, the waiting line to get them to deal with you properly may be unacceptably long. Should you then settle for a merely better practitioner? Of course, you should. Benchmarking is comparison for improvement. Some projects generate a *breakthrough*; most just give you substantial improvement or even a mere step up on your continuous improvement. The overall effort, however, is worthwhile by any measure.

MISCONCEPTIONS ABOUT BENCHMARKING

Many people think all benchmarking is competitive. How do we compare with our arch-rival(s)? This is important, of course, but extremely difficult to do with a sense of confidence in the result. Consultants and former employees of the competitors offer information. The competitors exaggerate in their press releases and captive magazine articles on the information they want you to know. But, what they are really planning and doing is top secret.

Look at it this way: The purpose of benchmarking is to make you better. If you do it well, you gain ground on the competitor, even if the reference point for setting goals is a compendium of how noncompetitors do things. That is why the definition above emphasizes *mutual* improvement. Everyone gains much better information in that manner.

Another major misconception is that benchmarking and performance measurement are essentially the same thing. This comes from the surveyor-oriented origins of the word. Here are some questions and definitions that will help you distinguish them from each other:

- Performance measurement: Is the organization improving in magnitude and direction intended?

- Benchmarking: Has the organization reached its potential levels as compared to other organizations?

- Benchmarking provides level/goal information to enhance performance trend measurement.

- Performance measurement provides the means of quantification for comparisons between organizations after analysis has assured fairness.

It is possible to locate an internal (usually historical) benchmark for volume, cost, quality, profit, or other aspect of performance, compare it to your own subsequent performance, then claim you are benchmarking. This is not benchmarking. It is simply performance trend measurement, a worthy but different thing. Benchmarking requires comparison with another organization.

BENCHMARKING AND MEASUREMENT

Performance measurement becomes a part of bench-marking. Once you clearly identify and chart a department or process, you can analyze it with measures of cost, quality, cycle time, and so on. The measure, however, is usually in terms of *level* of performance, not trend. Thus, measurement is a subset of benchmarking that provides quantification for comparable departments or processes. Benchmarking can, in turn, be considered a subset of measurement. It is the main technique for generating to supplement trend measurement and provide the basis for organizational goal-setting.

2

TYPES OF BENCHMARKING

The four major types of benchmarking project are:

- internal benchmarking

- industry study

- business process (exchange model)

- business process (group model)

INTERNAL BENCHMARKING

Most organizations do not get full value out of internal comparison possibilities. Though they have mutual-exchange meetings between counterparts from different divisions, product lines, and/or locations, these are rarely done systematically. It becomes too easy to dismiss the success story of another division by saying that one aspect of what they did is not relevant to the other division. If they analyze the story, however, they might well find that they could transfer most of the true innovations if they bypass the complicating detail.

Internal Benchmarking at IBM

IBM developed a form of internal benchmarking called the "Common Staffing Study" (CSS), which made simple comparisons across all plants and then across all corporate staffs around the world.[1] The comparisons used number of people assigned to a function versus an indicator of the magnitude of output of that function (number of invoice clerks versus number of invoices emitted). There are many valid reasons why organizations might differ in their staffing philosophies, but it is constructive that everyone understand and interpret these reasons to separate the valid from the invalid. IBM has gone on to much more sophisticated approaches to benchmarking, but the CSS got them started, and created in everyone the desire to make comparisons where possible on the reasonableness of what is being done or proposed.[2]

Internal Benchmarking and Small Organizations

It may be objected that small organizations cannot do internal benchmarking. This is true at the very small level, but many modest-sized organizations have several plants, regions, and/or offices that can be compared.

INDUSTRY STUDY

One of the more fruitful and cost-effective means of benchmarking is the cooperative industry study. The focus is to learn about your competitors, but in a general way rather than specifically. The conclusions are usually presented as *tendencies* of segments of the industry. These are based on averaging several responses or on heavily disguised individual company data. The subject matter is usually strategic rather than operational detail, although both appear frequently.

An industry study is organized by a trusted middleman, either an industry trade association or a specialized consultant. Data is gathered by survey, phone interview, and/or focus groups. The individual responses are kept confidential. The middleman is responsible for analyzing the data and coming to conclusions. The conclusions may be presented only to participants or, in some cases, released to the outside world without identifying the participants.

Issues that have been the subject of successful industry studies are:

- vertical integration/resource mix
- maintenance/support levels
- internal quality levels
- customer satisfaction results/costs
- equipment configuration/use
- personnel statistics/employee mix
- environmental policies/practices
- major equipment problems/costs

One risk of an industry study is that, especially in an oligopoly situation, the competitors start looking like each other and doing things the same way. If data is gathered on the maintenance policies of the eight dominant companies in an industry, for example, we may conclude that all companies are covered by a range of 2.5 to 4.0% of sales. In fact, it may be perfectly rational to invest 8.0% or 1.0% in certain circumstances. This might be the practice in a closely related industry or among smaller players in this industry. A multi-industry study, though it has other problems, gives you a wider window on the world.

Chapter 4 describes an industry study project in detail.

BUSINESS PROCESS: EXCHANGE MODEL

Much of the recent progress in benchmarking has been in using a two-organization exchange model, well-described in Camp's work.[3] In this model, an organization that desires to benchmark strategically analyzes its needs, then identifies the most interesting areas of study. The company then researches the issues using libraries, consultants, and clearinghouses to identify the best practitioners in the targeted business process, regardless of industry. The company negotiates with the potential partner to meet and to exchange carefully described data in a mutually agreed format.

An Example: Company A has decided Customer Complaint Handling is the critical business process it wants to improve. They identify Company B as the best practitioner of Customer Complaint Handling. Company B agrees to provide information on how they handle complaints if Company A, in turn, gives a similar level of information to Company B on how their Safety Program works. Thus, both companies gain. Since Company A and Company B are not competitors, neither is giving up corporate secrets to the competition.

Chapter 5 describes a project that uses this model.

BUSINESS PROCESS: GROUP MODEL

One problem with the exchange model is that it may be difficult to find a reciprocal subject that Company B needs and Company A has. An alternative approach for Company A to get its information is to hire a consultant or other neutral party to find several companies from different industries who are interested in Customer Complaint Handling. The neutral party analyzes and synthesizes how these organizations implement the process. This avoids the risk of wasting time and money if company B turns out not to be a good match for the exchange. By identifying several excellent companies who agree to participate (in the group model), the odds are good that one of them, or perhaps some combination of their approaches, truly represents the "best practice," especially if they represent many industries, approaches, and even nations. On the other hand, big money can be spent gathering all that information. And if the facilitating consultant is more of a peak-smoother than an innovator, then the result may be an expensive lowest common denominator!

3

SUBJECTS OF BENCHMARKING

Benchmarking can be done over a wide range of subjects:

- financial data

- nature of product/service

- operational practices

- process/department descriptions

- operational metrics

FINANCIAL DATA

Business magazines often sponsor huge studies that compare financial statistics, essentially a form of benchmarking. Sometimes they target one industry, and other times they include all industries.

Within an industry, it is reasonable to compare rates of growth and various types of return on investment over the long term. Increasingly, these have deteriorated to shorter time periods, and the proliferation of adjustments to earnings makes any organization's rating a function of how the analysts read the footnotes.

Another problem is industry membership. Many organizations prosper because their niche crosses traditional industry boundaries. Perhaps financial comparison tables give an ordinary company an idea of what it takes to become Wall-Street-famous in their industry, but those who know the industry in depth rely on "physical" data to make the final judgments. They want to know the target company's record in productivity, cycle times, quality improvement, safety, new products, research directions, and key market shares. We can benchmark these too, but only with the cooperation of the organizations involved.

Attempting to take isolated financial statistics across industries is worse than worthless. Each industry has its typical configurations of costs, leverage, market growth and inventory practice. To say, for example, that the 3M Corporation is $2\frac{1}{2}$ times better than WalMart because that is the proportion of their returns on sales is truly meaningless.

NATURE OF PRODUCT/SERVICE

The marketing research industry uses a well-established form of benchmarking: They have consumers compare features, costs, and longer-term performance results of competing products and services. We rarely recognize this as a form of benchmarking, because it is done quietly by outside experts rather than by the producing organizations themselves. As with other forms of benchmarking, the parties involved gather data with product/service improvement in mind, not just to have data.

OPERATIONAL PRACTICES/EQUIPMENT

Trade associations often poll their members on how they do certain things or what equipment they use. The responses to this form of benchmarking are typically binary: Do you have one of those (yes or no?), Do you make or buy?, Do you use distributors or direct-sell? These kinds of questions may be included in a survey that is partly financial information and partly general operating data.

PROCESS / DEPARTMENT DESCRIPTIONS

This is now mainstream benchmarking. For strategic planning purposes, it is good for the top of the organization to know that they are out of step in some things and basically sound in others. But the place where direct improvement action can take place is in the middle of the organization, through which all cross-cutting business processes thread. It is usually no simple matter to say who is best at doing the work at this level, because the work can be so different from organization to organization. One organization thinks customer complaint handling is simply paying off customers as soon as they say anything. Relatively few people are involved in this. The cycle time of "handling" is short, but the cost is very high. The pay-offs cost money, and very little data is gathered on how to prevent it from happening again.

Another organization assigns a small army to customer complaint handling. They analyze the validity of the customer's complaint, thus gathering useful information on where the system broke down. They come up with different ways of satisfying the customer, depending on the customer's needs, and they set up problem-solving teams to implement preventative corrections. This involves many people, has a longer cycle time, but probably costs a little less in the short run and a great deal less in the long run because it fixes the problems *and* prevents them in the future.

Which is the "best practice"? We can only begin to answer this question when we fully describe each way of doing the job in terms of inputs, deliverables, controls, and resources. This is the heart of benchmarking (and we haven't even gotten to numbers yet!).

OPERATIONAL METRICS

Much benchmarking starts out to be an exercise in comparing numbers. Once process and/or department descriptions are laid out and adjusted, it then becomes possible to compare numbers intelligently to see who is best. But we still have to say *what* is best.

Below are lists of categories of measures with numerous examples that might be part of a comparison project. The situation usually dictates what measures represent the important issues, but different observers emphasize different measures.

QUALITY

- error rate, rework

- unintended scrap/waste

- variation reduction

- cost of (poor) quality

- customer satisfaction survey results

- returns/warranty cost

- service quality level

- emission level/pollutants

COST/PRODUCTIVITY

- labor productivity

- energy productivity

- materials yield

- inventory turnover

- cost of service

- designed interruptions in process flow

- utilization of fixed resources
- number of process steps

TIMELINESS

- on-time delivery
- cycle time, customer view
- cycle time, in-shop
- documentation timeliness

GENERAL EFFECTIVENESS

- safety
- employee attitude
- creativity
- team effectiveness/participation
- new products/services
- housekeeping/cleanliness
- employee skill mix
- market success

Most "best" candidates satisfy their customers first. Most customers want quality first. ("It works." "It is what I ordered/expected.") So, measures of quality are part of most benchmarking projects. Rivaling quality are *cost* and *timeliness*. Cost may not play much of a role in comparing heart surgery suppliers, but it dominates the choice of commodity food or chemical products. Timeliness surpasses even quality with some parts supplies to assembly manufacturers, but may be way down the list with some noncritical construction projects.

Still other factors may determine who's best in some other special applications. Ad agencies are differentiated by their creativity. Some maintenance operations are dead without good/prompt documentation. For some sensitive-environment manufacturing, cleanliness/housekeeping is a key requirement. Gunpowder manufacturers had better consider safety. Airlines need energy productivity. Some retail businesses are most affected by inventory turnover.

Benchmarking may appear to be about metrics, but a great deal of behind-the-scenes thinking is required to make comparisons fair and to choose exactly the right parameters before nominating the "best."

4

BENCHMARKING EXAMPLE: INDUSTRY STUDY

An industry study is usually organized by an interested but neutral party. In many countries a government or quasi-governmental entity sponsors comparison studies between firms in an industry. Their prime objective is to gather information to use in their industrial policy formulations and adjustments. The worst of these are the political rationalizations for a predetermined policy shift. The best of these are honest attempts to see how to help a domestic industry compete internationally or how regulations might improve the dynamics of domestic competition.

The better studies are often those that are organized routinely, rather than in response to a special problem or plea. The prime objective of these studies is to give "strategic profile" information so industry participants can more intelligently help themselves to compete by lowering costs, improving quality, or better satisfying special customer needs. The Canadian government provides an excellent example. The Industry Canada Department of the federal government selects industries for their studies and then asks for voluntary and confidential participation from the firms in that industry. Each firm is visited by an Industry Canada representative who gathers financial and physical data that pertains to their operations. Approximately 25 to 40 performance ratios are calculated from that data for each firm and the industry median is determined. Each firm receives a unique report on their relative position and an interpretive visit. The industry as a whole and the parts of the government concerned with industrial policy receive the aggregated but disguised report containing all the data. Eighty-five industries and 2,700 companies have participated in this program to date.[4]

Potential nongovernmental sponsors include trade and professional associations, private nonprofit productivity centers or research organizations, specialized consultants, and regional economic development centers. They all share a knowledge of the industry in question. They are also in positions of adequate trust. This assures the main industry organizations who participate that sensitive information will be kept confidential. It also helps if the sponsoring organization can manage the project and its funding smoothly.

FINDING PARTICIPANTS

The original hurdle any organizer faces is to convince some of the more secretive industry leaders that they can gain by participating. "Help your competitors" is not a very good rallying cry! But beating a new foreign competitor industry or a substitute-product industry (metal cans for glass) might serve. Even without an external threat, the industry's collective bankers, for example, would like the whole industry to operate on a higher plane even if the relative positions of market share stay the same. Also, in some industries, such as electric utilities or bread baking, the organizations are mainly regional and do not all compete with each other in the traditional sense.

PLANNING THE STUDY

Once an organization decides to conduct such a study, the first step is to get technical help to plan the study, with emphasis on the means of gathering and interpreting the data. Some sponsoring organizations already have the technical basis in the industry and in productivity and quality concepts. Others have to bring in an outsider acceptable to everyone. Most sponsoring organizations set up a special committee of industry leaders to find the technical help, plan the contact with potential participants, and direct the study as it proceeds.

The selected technical specialist typically spends time with the committee, using it as a sounding board for determining how to gather the data and what data to gather. The specialist then usually gathers data by asking participants to fill out a questionnaire and return it to the sponsoring organization or to the neutral technical specialist. In the case of a small group of organizations engaged in a complex business, consultants might travel to the participants' locations and help them fill out the questionnaire. Smaller groups can also use focus groups or other interviewing techniques to supplement and/or replace a mail survey.

SURVEY DEVELOPMENT

The committee and specialists who develop the survey need to decide the following:

- who to survey (members, customers, several categories)

- what kind of data to ask for (available/weak or unavailable/strong)

- what to find out (facts, ratios, opinions, strategies)

- time period of data

- physical and/or financial data

- participant categories
- marketing of survey (due date, length, graphics, endorsements)

There is usually a trade-off between using readily available data and the data that is needed but less available. A relatively trusted sponsoring organization can be more ambitious in this regard than a newcomer. A newcomer may take a tiered approach. They can make moderately useful conclusions from readily available data on a first survey. Then, when transmitting those results, or a few months later, they can propose a follow-up survey to develop more challenging data. "Forcing" the industry to develop this new data may turn out to be an important unforseen benefit for the industry.

Survey Participants

Choosing participants for the survey also raises some issues. An association sponsor tends to choose only members. On some issues, however, it may be important to include suppliers, customers, industry financial analysts, reporters covering the industry, regulators, union representatives, community leaders, and so on. Many associations have Associate Members who are suppliers to the main industry or are in a specialized segment. If you include them, some of the wording may need to be more general; you may need to add special sections to the survey; or you may need more than one survey format.

Survey Results

Surveys can generate many types of results. In some cases, they emphasize simple fact-finding with yes/no questions. In other cases, the survey gathers data in a relatively raw form. A survey processor then calculates ratios of performance or characteristics, based on the raw data. Sometimes, in addition to benchmarking comparisons, a survey also gathers opinions on legislation, equipment design, management practices, and so on. There are some strategies that can be asked about directly with yes/no questions, such as make-to-stock or to-order, eliminating inspection, preventive maintenance. Others must be inferred, such as degree of customer responsiveness or attention to technology.

Survey Data

The time period of the data is important. Some questions concern current practices, but others require data from the latest reporting period or a specific month, quarter, or year. The questions must be absolutely clear or some of the responses will be unusable. As a general rule, physical data is more useful for diagnosis than financial data, but financial data may be more readily available. If the survey uses financial data, and, if you are looking for improvement trends, be sure to remove the inflationary effects before drawing conclusions. If the survey uses physical data, be careful of merging unlike units, whether they are units of output, accomplishment, or headcount. It may be worth the trouble to gather data at a more detailed level than you need to protect against "mix shift" or other weighting issues.

Along with information that pertains to productivity, quality, cycle time, and other data being analyzed, it is necessary to find out where the repondent fits in several sorted categories. Below is a list of many of these categories. (The most important are usually *size of organization, detailed nature of product, market segment*, and *geographic region*.)

- type of product or material

- type of packaging or format

- size of product/service

- geographic region

- company/division size

- plant size

- key equipment used

- key equipment age/capacity

- market(s) sold to

- type(s) of fuel used

- population density

- maintenance policy

- degree of vertical integration (buy or make components)

- make for stock or order

- worker profile

- existence of "quality" program

Be careful also about the length of the survey and the return date. A survey that is longer than four pages, folded over, is likely to be thrown away rather than answered. Precede longer surveys by a letter (under separate cover) from the most notable person possible as to why response is the only sane option! Include clear advice on who in the typical organization is best postioned to answer the questions. The deadline should be two to three weeks after expected receipt of the survey mailing. This should be enough time to gather the data, but not enough to allow the recipient to put it off until later. Good graphics, clear and eye-catching, help, but are not enough. Test the survey on a few of the target recipients to see what problems they have. Parkinson's Laws exist mainly for those who write surveys!

PROCESSING AND INTERPRETATION

Participants can return completed surveys to the sponsoring group or the assisting specialist. Or, the sponsor can develop a double-blind system to ensure complete confidentiality.[5] It is good to maintain a track to each respondent through a double-blind type of system so you can check and revise "absurd" data if necessary, rather than reject that participant. It is very easy to misplace decimal points or use data from the wrong time period (month vs. quarter).

Reporting Results

The most powerful method of reporting is to report the overall industry results and inferences to the whole body of participants, the whole group of association members, or even the whole world. But each participant also wants a private report on how they stand relative to the rest of industry. This is easy to do, as long as you retain the track to the participant and the budget takes the extra work into account.

In public meetings, absolutely no one admits to being below average in anything, but it is likely that almost half of the group is below average overall, and *everyone* is below average in something. The private individual reports thus provide at least some shock value and stimulus to do things differently.

If the survey becomes an annual event, the value expands greatly, because *level* data can be supplemented with *trend* data. This can include who is best or worst, and who is doing something about it! Table 1 shows a generic industry report. Table 2 presents the type of report that an individual participant could receive, even in the first year of participation.

perception of the results of a certain process while lowering personnel costs at least 10 percent).

The Benchmarking Team

During the planning exercise participants probably identified a process owner who will establish a team to make the study and implement the recommendations. Below is a list of some business processes that have been the focus of benchmarking projects.

- concurrent engineering
- individual performance appraisal
- after-sales service
- software quality review
- customer complaint handling
- new product development administration
- cycle time reduction methodology
- patent applications
- customer requirements setting
- supplier certification
- customer satisfaction measurement
- machine tool setup
- training needs analysis

A successful benchmarking team does not have to include only high-powered people. In fact, the best teams are made up from a diagonal slice of the organization that includes people from various parts and levels. The team needs a high-level sponsor to ensure that the team gets the proper resources, entries, and exemptions, but the team should include many of the people who actually do the work being studied. They know the truth about how they are accomplishing the process now, and their cooperation (enthusiasm, if possible) is necessary when it comes time to install the modified process or approach. If they have had some influence and responsibility in designing the new process, they will be much better at conveying the new approach to their coworkers with genuine enthusiasm.

An effective benchmarking team also needs some technical expertise and/or previous training. The team should contain at least one person with flowcharting skills, some people with good interviewing skills, at least one person familiar with the accounting systems of the company, a good meeting facilitator (this can be an outside consultant), and someone familiar with the customers' needs and methods of operating. Skill in using computers, writing, and graphics also helps in the various levels of presentations that are needed. Below is a list of possible training topics for the team after it is formed:

- the nature of a process, systems, flowcharts

- team behavior, meeting skills, interviewing, negotiating

- technical content of target process

- legal considerations in "going outside"

- basics of performance measurement, cost accounting

- computer use: on-line data bases, graphics, note-taking

It is also necessary that the members of the new benchmarking team have time to do the project work. Senior executives and renowned technical specialists would become bottlenecks in scheduling the team's work.

Benchmarking Issues

Most of the issues that benchmarking addresses are not profound. They may be subtle or tricky, but any person who thinks about them can understand and contibute to these issues. In fact, the best benchmarking projects are those in which a company completely reinterprets the customer's needs and/or the best way to meet those needs. The required intellectual flexibility may well be found among people who have not "done this sort of thing" before.

Benchmarking Time Frames

The time requirement for benchmarking teams varies with the size of the process chosen and the deadlines imposed. Some successful benchmarkers have assigned a full-time team and have the project completed in three or four months. Others plan a one-day-per-week meeting, and the project requires nine to twelve months. Other variations are full-time leader/analyst and part-time team; full-time benchmarking specialist participating in three projects; three full-time project leaders and part-time team members.

INFORMATION BASE

Once the topic is selected and the team is organized, there are two distinct types of preparatory activities required. They are often done in parallel, splitting the team into two subteams for more efficient coordination.

Researching the Process Externally

One subteam looks outside the immediate organization and gathers information on how others do the process they are studying. Some of this is formal library research and data-base search, gathering printed words from the public domain. There is much more of that than most people realize.[6] Not only do the generic business magazines directly put out much information on best practices, but also much information is buried in stories on an organization where the main theme is not significantly related to the benchmarking topic. Trade magazines and newspapers do not specialize in management issues, but they can include some articles for breadth or mention management issues in passing while discussing technical tools or product characteristics. Wall Street analysts both hear and make presentations. Consultants and marketing research groups conduct studies. Some industries bury a lot of information in tedious regulatory reports.

This subteam should not just read. Talking to industry associations, consultants, bankers, your employees who have worked elsewhere, and community associations, or even neighbors can be fruitful in some cases. Interviewing journalists who have written the most useful and relevant articles is the best single "sure thing." Much more useful and specific information is left on the cutting-room floor than was put in the article, and most reporters can add their own subjective judgement to the more hedged material they published.

Researching the Process Internally

While one subteam is out researching the public domain, the other is gathering information about how the organization does the work now. This is more difficult than it sounds. A visit to the procedures manual is a good idea, but it may not reflect many of the informal and undocumented changes the process has gone through over the years. Some of the most interesting and fruitful projects deal with business processes that are relatively new and/or cut across many departments in a subtle manner. Here the procedures manual may not even recognize the existence of that process. The manual may also treat it as a series of mechanical handoffs from department to department rather than the chaotic, but cooperative, "fire drill" it has become.

Another problem (actually opportunity) is that different departments may perform the process differently. It is important to document and compare all these methods to arrive at the best one or few internal approaches before anyone talks very much to any outside organizations about comparison.

The next section, on the process template, outlines the information to gather. The focus is on flowcharts of all process alternatives along with data on the cost, time, and type of result for each approach. Also, the outline includes information on who owns the process and how it is managed (if it is).

The two subteams then present their findings to each other, and they will find a great deal of overlap. What one article discussed is actually being installed in one remote part of this organization. The approach that *Industry Week* joked about is exactly how we do it at headquarters! The consultant who said the relevant range of cycle times is three to four days needs to be questioned further as to inputs and ouputs, because the best we can do is five days. One company actually claims to do it without any inspection — how is that possible?

The above is the raw material for a plan of how to proceed to the outside world.

PROCESS TEMPLATE

Many of the ways practices differ between organizations involve scope and intent rather than ways of doing a certain type of work. Once organizations address scope and intent issues, a fair comparison is possible between different ways of doing the same work. The following is a list of the main kinds of information to gather:

- definition and boundaries
- inputs
- outputs
- ownership
- participants
- measures
- inspections/reviews
- improvement in progress
- subprocesses
- previous benchmarks

To help gather this information, ask the following questions for each category:

Definition and boundaries. What exactly do different key players call the target process? Where does it begin, where does it end, and where is it physically located?

Inputs. What resources are present at the starting point? What materials are received? What information is needed? From whom is energy or capital required? Can the process be done with either "less finished" or "more finished" components?

Outputs. What is delivered from this process and to whom? Is the product/service different with different customers? Are there different degrees of "finish" or different levels of quality specified and/or tolerated? Is the output called different things by different people?

Ownership. Each relevant department has a department manager. For processes that cut across several departments, who takes the lead on issues that concern the effectiveness of that process? Also does the organization have a "czar" for that subject who knows the most about the process regardless of formal reporting relationships?

Participants. What parts of what departments are assigned to the process (or act as if they are so assigned)? Who else is critical to the process as a supplier, customer, advisor, inspector, reviewer, auditor, and so on? Do the human resources vary with the type of product/service or nature of customer?

Measures. How is the process now measured within the relevant departments? How is the process measured as a whole? What is the performance trend in those measures? Are there any level measures? Which measures does the company currently use? Which could be used if they were available or desirable? Are the measures technically sound (weighting soundness, inflation adjustment, farmouts, target point vs. control range, etc)?

Inspections and reviews. How often does the company halt, divert, or otherwise intervene in the process for inspection and review? Is this required by customer, procedures manual, informal practice, or executive decree? Would the company/process gain any cycle time if they canceled the practice, or was that dead time anyhow? Who does the reviewing/inspecting and does it vary depending on the person?

Improvement in progress. Are you dealing with a "moving target" here? What is driving the company to change the current method? Can you stop it or integrate it with the benchmarking project? Who is doing the improvement work?

Defined subprocesses. Once interviews and work in the field have defined the target process, can you separately analyze the natural subprocesses involved? Are the subprocesses the same at each location organizationally? What is the breakdown on cost, people, time, and error rate per subprocess? Is there a Pareto conclusion here?

Previous benchmarks. Are there any "everyone knows" type of statements that lead to formal or informal goals/targets dating from the past? What is their source and justification? Can you change or erase them?

OUTSIDE COMPARISONS

The research has probably shown that plenty of information is now available on how the organization performs the process and what the outside world has to say about that type of work. It is now time to find an "exchange" benchmarking partner outside the organization. The team might have done this in parallel with the above research. Executive intuition might have already identified the process to benchmark as well as the company to benchmark with, or library research might have already suggested an obvious partner with apparently excellent practices in the target area. Regardless, an appropriately high-ranking executive must be the one to approach the most interesting potential partner. The team might arrange a meeting of the sponsoring executive and the project leader with their counterparts at the target organization.

Preparation

If the target organization has not been itself preparing for a mutual benchmarking project, they may need some time to think through what they want from you. You then, will probably need time to develop your side of the subject they suggest. The target organization also needs to formalize their excellent process. This usually is not a problem. One of the attributes of an excellent process is that it is quite simple and transparent. You would not have heard about it unless they had been talking about it, which in turn required some preparation on their part. Identifying the best partner early in the research gives them more time to prepare and can prevent delay to your project. On the other hand, it is not wise to cut the internal analysis project short because you can learn so much that is of permanent value. Nor is it wise to cut the library work short, because there is always a chance this partner cannot provide a usable approach and you'll have to choose a second partner.

Ground Rules

An early and necessary part of the external project is to come to an agreement with the outsiders on general conduct of the study. Many organizations, unfortunately, choose to admit lawyers to the project at this point. What the partners need most at this point, however, is ground rules rather than strict procedures and prohibitions. Usually the participating organizations are not competitors. They may have previously cooperated as supplier and customer. They may be geographic neighbors. They may share a minority owner or an investment banker. Or they may have no previous relationship. A benchmarking code of conduct was developed by the International Benchmarking Clearinghouse of the American Productivity & Quality Center. Most of the issues are more concerned with common courtesy than with legal issues.

BENCHMARKING CODE OF CONDUCT

- Conduct yourself within legal bounds.
- Participate by exchanging information.
- Respect confidentiality of information.
- Use information only for the intended purpose.
- Initiate contacts with designated individuals.
- Obtain permission before providing contacts.
- Be prepared for each benchmarking event.
- Follow through with commitments to partners.
- Treat information from others as they desire.

Source: International Benchmarking Clearinghouse

The two parties also have to decide if they want neutral facilitation or whether the two team leaders or someone else can handle it. They have to decide at what point visitation becomes important. At one extreme is the highly visible production process that you have to see to talk about it. At the other extreme is a computer-based support process or production process apparent only through the morale of the workers and the computers they use. If in doubt, delay site visits until the participants understand not only what is happening, but also what is supposed to be happening, and how this looks on measurement charts and tables.

Comparing Approaches

Once the teams from both organizations have done their ground work, they need to present their approaches to each other. This meeting, or series of meetings, can last for minutes, hours, or days. The teams need to compare, contrast, challenge, and generally clarify for the originating team how they might use what they learned from the approach of the target team/organization. Sometimes this is of little value. The target organization might have a special circumstance, customer quirk, or unique equipment that is difficult for the originating organization to reproduce. The target organization usually agrees to present and discuss their approach, but usually not to help in the installation of the new approach, even if it is fully acceptable.

Accepting the Approach

So the originating team has to return home, contemplate what they learned, and then either proceed to more benchmarking or to the development of an installation/implementation project. The returning team usually only makes a recommendation. It is up to the sponsoring executive(s) to decide whether to accept and proceed or not. Much of the discussion revolves around proforma goal setting. For example, they currently might be producing at $456 per shot, with a 5.3 percent error rate, and a lead time of six weeks. Their goal for next year was to be producing at $425 per shot, 4.5 percent error rate, and a five-week lead time, although it was not clear how they would achieve this. Now this (crazy?) team comes back and says they can do it for less than $100 per shot, 1.0 percent error rate, and lead time of one week initially, and, later, two days. To pull this off requires changing some previously sacred work rules, so the union has to agree (Fortunately two people on the team were union members.) They would need to buy more versatile and lighter-weight machinery. And, they would need to convince some of their customers to receive the product in different packaging. This has become a complex decision!

IMPLEMENTING CHANGE

But now the good news: The venture created a very substantial improvement project without the large cost of a consultant's formal study. The proposed changes work elsewhere; so they do not have to be the pioneers. Many of the recommending team are familiar with both the old way and new way of doing things; this is certainly a first around here! All the departments were involved, the union was involved, and someone else, in addition to the accountants and engineers, was working with the numbers. It sounds like a good chance for success, and they now have some experienced benchmarkers who can move on to other process teams. They incurred some cost to provide information on their other process to the partner company. But even here they might learn something new. Once the benchmarking team provides its recommendations for change, two cautions are worth mentioning:

- Several stakeholders are watching with some apprehension, unless the company brought them into the project earlier. The process owner and some of the people in the current process, hopefully, were involved in the project and received the proper assurances about employment security and a chance to influence the current solution. If not, provide this groundwork before the installation project begins.

- If the benchmarking affects outside customers and suppliers, they also should have been on the project early. Their opinions are valuable and they also need proper assurances that the improvement benefits them as well. They need to know that the company will correct any problem.

Finally, the rhetoric of change needs to emphasize that this is one in a series of ongoing changes rather than the final solution for all time. Most benchmarking organizations recognize the need for periodic strategic reviews every few years of previously benchmarked subjects. Reviews guard against lapses into the "old way" and encourage the realization that an even better way can be developed at any time, especially as corporate strategies change.[7]

6

SUMMARY

Benchmarking is systematic comparison between organizations. Anyone can benchmark with anyone, but the search is for *best* practices, so the demand is on high-reputation companies. The meaning of 'best' varies widely — it can be lowest cost, highest perceived quality, lowest actual error rate or waste, shortest cycle time, or other variables or combinations.

Organizations can benchmark internally, within an industry, or outside an industry. The issues in question can be strategic or operational, industry-specific or quite generic. Studies can involve two organizations, several organizations, or a whole industry or category.

Regardless of the subject, the organization, or the format, benchmarking outreach and comparison provide several substantial advantages:

The goal-setting process gains objectivity. The organization sees evidence of what others can do and accepts goals more readily because they are more realistic.

An organization examines itself. The pressure of giving information on itself to outsiders makes an organization think seriously about how it does things. Fact replaces hunch. Measures replace vague words.

Benchmarking teams become effective change agents. Given cross-cutting responsibility, they carry an issue through from definition, to discovery, to implementation.

Benchmarking increases profits. Officially the teams were developed to make substantial improvements or breakthroughs. Sometimes this happens, but sometimes the improvement is more modest on any one process or strategic issue. An overall benchmarking program, however, employs several different appropriate approaches, which makes it a high-yield project in money terms!

NOTES

1. Conway, David L., "Common Staffing System," in *White Collar Productivity*, edited by Robert N. Lehrer (New York: McGraw-Hill, 1983), 181–200.

2. Balm, Gerald, *Benchmarking: A Practitioner's Guide* (Schaumburg, IL: QPMA Press, 1992). Balm draws from his experience at IBM Rochester, MN.

3. Camp, Robert C., *Benchmarking* (Milwaukee: Quality Press, 1989).

4. Canadian Interfirm Comparison Program is described in W. Christopher and Carl G. Thor (eds.), *Handbook for Productivity Measurement and Improvement* (Portland, Ore.: Productivity Press, 1993).

5. A double-blind system lets one neutral party mail and receive the survey in sealed envelopes. Another neutral party opens the sealed envelopes of data and handles data entry and analysis of what is to them anonymous data.

6. The International Benchmarking Clearinghouse of the American Productivity & Quality Center in Houston, Texas was organized to provide library and partner-matching services of the type described. They provide many services for nonmembers in addition to "turnkey" benchmarking help for members, including an asynchronous computer network exclusively for benchmarking specialists and a variety of training courses.

7. The relation of benchmarking and strategic planning is best discussed in Gregory H. Watson, *Strategic Benchmarking* (New York: Wiley and Sons, 1993), and the introduction to *The Benchmarking Workbook* (Portland, Ore.: Productivity Press, 1992).

FURTHER READING

American Productivity & Quality Center, *Benchmarking Management Guide* (Houston: APQC, 1993).

American Productivity & Quality Center, *Benchmarking the Best* (Houston: APQC, 1993), award-winning case studies.

Gerald Balm, *Benchmarking: A Practitioner's Guide* (Schaumburg, Ill.: QPMA Press, 1992), experiences at IBM.

Robert C. Camp, *Benchmarking: Search for Industry Best Practices* (Milwaukee: Quality Press, 1989), the "classic," Xerox's experiences.

C.J. McNair and Kathleen Leibfried, *Benchmarking: Tool for Continuous Improvement* (New York: Harper Business, 1992).

Michael J. Spendolini, *The Benchmarking Book* (New York: AMACOM, 1992).

Gregory H. Watson, *The Benchmarking Workbook* (Portland, Ore.: Productivity Press, 1992).

————, *Strategic Benchmarking* (New York: John Wiley and Sons, 1993).

ABOUT THE AUTHOR

Carl G. Thor is president of Jarrett Thor International. Previously he served as president and vice chairman of the American Productivity & Quality Center, responsible for productivity measurement and gainsharing. Earlier positions were with Anderson Clayton and Humble Oil. He has led industry studies and statistical research projects, conducted workshops, authored many articles, and is contributing author and coeditor of the *Handbook for Productivity Measurement and Improvement*, and author of *Doing and Rewarding: Inside a High-Performance Organization*, volume 6 of the Management Master Series.

Carl G. Thor, Jarrett Thor International, 771 Battery Place, Alexandria, VA 22314.

The Management Master Series

The *Management Master Series* offers business managers leading-edge information on the best contemporary management practices. Written by highly respected authorities, each short "briefcase book" addresses a specific topic in a concise, to-the-point presentation, using both text and illustrations. These are ideal books for busy managers who want to get the whole message quickly.

Set 1 — Great Management Ideas

1. ***Management Alert: Don't Reform—Transform!***
   Michael J. Kami

   Transform your corporation: adapt faster, be more productive, perform better.

2. ***Vision, Mission, Total Quality: Leadership Tools for Turbulent Times***
   William F. Christopher

   Build your vision and mission to achieve world class goals.

3. ***The Power of Strategic Partnering***
   Eberhard E. Scheuing

   Take advantage of the strengths in your customer-supplier chain.

4. ***New Performance Measures***
   Brian H. Maskell

   Measure service, quality, and flexibility with methods that address your customers' needs.

5. ***Motivating Superior Performance***
   Saul W. Gellerman

   Use these key factors—nonmonetary as well as monetary—to improve employee performance.

6. ***Doing and Rewarding: Inside a High-Performance Organization***
   Carl G. Thor

   Design systems to reward superior performance and encourage productivity.

PRODUCTIVITY PRESS, Dept. BK, PO Box 13390, Portland, OR 97213-0390
Phone (503) 235-0600   Fax (503) 235-0909

Set 2 — Total Quality

7. *The 16-Point Strategy for Productivity and Total Quality*
   William F. Christopher and Carl G. Thor

   Essential points you need to know to improve the performance of your organization.

8. *The TQM Paradigm: Key Ideas That Make It Work*
   Derm Barrett

   Get a firm grasp of the world-changing ideas behind the Total Quality movement.

9. *Process Management: A Systems Approach to Total Quality*
   Eugene H. Melan

   Learn how a business process orientation will clarify and streamline your organization's capabilities.

10. *Practical Benchmarking for Mutual Improvement*
    Carl G. Thor

    Discover a down-to-earth approach to benchmarking and building useful partnerships for quality.

11. *Mistake-Proofing: Designing Errors Out*
    Richard B. Chase and Douglas M. Stewart

    Learn how to eliminate errors and defects at the source with inexpensive poka-yoke devices and staff creativity.

12. *Communicating, Training, and Developing for Quality Performance*
    Saul W. Gellerman

    Gain quick expertise in communication and employee development basics.

These books are sold in sets. Each set is $85.00 plus $5.00 shipping and handling. Future sets will cover such topics as Customer Service, Leadership, and Innovation. For complete details, call 800-394-6868 or fax 800-394-6286.

PRODUCTIVITY PRESS, Dept. BK, PO Box 13390, Portland, OR 97213-0390
Phone (503) 235-0600   Fax (503) 235-0909

BOOKS FROM PRODUCTIVITY PRESS

Productivity Press provides individuals and companies with materials they need to achieve excellence in quality, productivity, and the creative involvement of all employees. Through sets of learning tools and techniques, Productivity supports continuous improvement as a vision, and as a strategy. Many of our leading-edge products are direct source materials translated into English for the first time from industrial leaders around the world. Call toll-free 1-800-394-6868 for our free catalog.

The Benchmarking Management Guide
American Productivity & Quality Center
If you're planning, organizing, or actually undertaking a benchmarking program, you need the most authoritative source of information to help you get started and to manage the process all the way through. Written expressly for managers of benchmarking projects by the APQC's renowned International Benchmarking Clearinghouse, this guide provides exclusive information on training courses and ways to apply Baldrige, Deming, and ISO 9000 criteria for internal assessment, and has a complete bibliography of benchmarking literature.
ISBN 1-56327-045-5 / 260 pages / $40.00 / Order BMG-B245

A New American TQM
Four Practical Revolutions in Management
Shoji Shiba, Alan Graham, and David Walden
For TQM to succeed in America, you need to create an American-style "learning organization" with the full commitment and understanding of senior managers and executives. Written expressly for this audience, *A New American TQM* offers a comprehensive and detailed explanation of TQM and how to implement it, based on courses taught at MIT's Sloan School of Management and the Center for Quality Management, a consortium of American companies. Full of case studies and amply illustrated, the book examines major quality tools and how they are being used by the most progressive American companies today.
ISBN 1-56327-032-3 / 606 pages / $50.00 / Order NATQM-B245

PRODUCTIVITY PRESS, Dept. BK, PO Box 13390, Portland, OR 97213-0390
Phone (503) 235-0600   Fax (503) 235-0909

The Benchmarking Workbook
Adapting Best Practices for Performance Improvement
Gregory H. Watson
Managers today need benchmarking to anticipate trends and maintain competitive advantage. This practical workbook shows you how to do your own benchmarking study. Watson's discussion includes a case study that takes you through each step of the benchmarking process, raises thought-provoking questions, and provides examples of how to use forms for a benchmarking study.
ISBN 1-56327-033-1 / 169 pages / $30.00 / Order BENCHW-B245

20 Keys to Workplace Improvement
Iwao Kobayashi
This easy-to-read introduction to the "20 keys" system presents an integrated approach to assessing and improving your company's competitive level. The book focuses on systematic improvement through five levels of achievement in such primary areas as industrial housekeeping, small group activities, quick changeover techniques, equipment maintenance, and computerization. A scoring guide is included, along with information to help plan a strategy for your company's world class improvement effort.
ISBN 1-915299-61-5 / 252 pages / $45.00 / Order 20KEYS-B245

TO ORDER: Write, phone, or fax Productivity Press, Dept. BK, P.O. Box 13390, Portland, OR 97213-0390, phone 1-800-394-6868, fax 1-800-394-6286. Send check or charge to your credit card (American Express, Visa, MasterCard accepted).

U.S. ORDERS: Add $5 shipping for first book, $2 each additional for UPS surface delivery. We offer attractive quantity discounts for bulk purchases of individual titles; call for more information.

INTERNATIONAL ORDERS: Write, phone, or fax for quote and indicate shipping method desired. For international callers, telephone number is 503-235-0600 and fax number is 503-235-0909. Prepayment in U.S. dollars must accompany your order (checks must be drawn on U.S. banks). When quote is returned with payment, your order will be shipped promptly by the method requested.

NOTE: Prices are in U.S. dollars and are subject to change without notice.

PRODUCTIVITY PRESS, Dept. BK, PO Box 13390, Portland, OR 97213-0390
Phone (503) 235-0600   Fax (503) 235-0909

NOTES

NOTES

NOTES

NOTES